Rules of Finance for Small Businesses

Pragmatic Publishing

Educational Press
Kingston, Jamaica

Rules of Finance for Small Businesses

Pragmatic Publishing

Is a division of

Pragmatic Productions Limited

This is part of the education arm of the company
That is concerned with the furtherance of education
and training.

Published in Jamaica
This Edition: 2016

ACKNOWLEDGEMENTS AND APPRECIATION

We would like to register our appreciation to the persons who have helped in the production of this book. To the hundreds of small business students who we have trained over the years and to our many clients, we would like to say thanks. To our spouses who have read through and have given us their criticisms, we would like to say thanks. To our children who have had time robbed from them because of this worthwhile project, we want to extend gratitude for your patience.

There are also those random persons with whom we have had various discussions about business. You have also contributed to the motivation to get this book off the press and into the hands of business owners and operators. Also we would like to say thanks to the various bankers with whom we have had the pleasure and displeasure of dealing with, whether it was for our own purpose or for that of our various clients. You have contributed to our knowledge and understanding of how this banks and other financial institutions interact with this sector.

DEDICATION

This book is dedicated to members of our families and to our students, past and future. Without you, this book would not have been connected to us because it is you who motivated it.

Paul O. Beale & Barry W. Robinson

Paul O. Beale

Paul O. Beale is a former lecturer in Business Management and marketing at UWI (School of Continuing Studies) and the University of Technology. He also attended these institutions in pursuit of his own qualifications in marketing, finance, small business management and managerial accounting. During the stint of lecturing, Mr. Beale would have taught thousands of students including business owners, business operators and persons who needed training in personal finance.

Mr. Beale also worked with H.E.A.R.T. Trust/NTA as a budgeting manager and Sector Specialist, at COK as a project analyst and at Caribbean Business Management Limited also as a project analyst. He holds a Post Graduate diploma in Marketing from the Chartered Institute of Marketing along with other qualifications from The UWI and Utech.

Mr. Beale currently holds the position of CEO for two companies, one in entertainment and the other in publishing and merchandising. He is also film editor, playwright, screenwriter, film director, author and trainer.

Barry W. Robinson

Barry W. Robinson is a Management Consultant whose experience locally and regionally spans over thirty years and covers a range of assignments in the public and private sectors.

Prior to becoming an independent consultant he has held senior and executive positions in public and private institutions in Jamaica and the United States. He held positions at the National Water Commission. He also held a senior position at Caribe Corporation USA. He would eventually open his own management consultant firm and that would have worked with a host of companies and individuals on a wide range of projects for both local and overseas organizations to include government departments.

During the past eighteen years, Mr. Robinson has been engaged in lecturing at the tertiary level both at the University of the West Indies and the University of Technology. His involvement in education consists of development and delivery of a number of courses in Small Business Management, Managerial Economics, Financial Management and Management accounting, Marketing and Entrepreneurship.

Mr. Robinson gained an M.B.A in Finance and Management from Marshall University, Huntington, West Virginia, 1977. BSc.- Business Administration from Montclair University New Jersey. 1974. He has completed post-graduate studies at Bradford University, United Kingdom, The Mona School of Business University of the West Indies in Corporate Planning and Marketing.

RULES ON FINANCE FOR SMALL BUSINESSES

Introduction

A business is essentially a system of commercial activities that revolves around income and expenditure. The end result of all these activities is either a profit or a loss. It is reasonable to assume that the main objective of a small business operator is to make a profit. That assumption is the foundation of the rules that have been laid out in this book.

A business has many facets to it and marketing and finance are the two most important. Marketing is the identification of consumer needs and wants, the development of products and services that will satisfy those needs and wants and to allow the subsequent distribution of these products and services at a profit or in a manner that allows the business to continue the provision of these products and services over time. That is a pretty comprehensive definition, but so too is the marketing function.

Finance, on the other hand, is the management of capital, expenses and revenues with the ultimate aim of achieving a surplus of revenues over expenses and to ensure viability of the business throughout the life cycle of the business.

From those two definitions, one thing is very clear. Marketing and finance exist in a symbiotic relationship. This means that these two operations depend on each other for the success of the business, similarly to how the heart and the brain work together for the body to operate optimally. In this manual, we will focus on finance, more specifically, the Thirty (33) rules of finance for small businesses.

Small businesses in Jamaica suffer from a number of problems, most of which are some as other businesses around the world. Some of these problems are due to the shortcomings of government policies while others are due to the inadequacies of the small business operators and owners. These problems include; challenging economic circumstances, the lack of business training, lack of knowledge about sources and types of funding, improper use of funds, poor marketing, poor planning and poor financial management.

The purpose of this book is to provide a guide for the avoidance of some of the aforementioned pitfalls or the management of the challenges that are inevitable. These guidelines are put forward in the form of rules accompanied by thorough explanations and applicability of these rules. This format was chosen to ensure that the reader focuses on one specific issue at a time.

However, while each of these rules must be taken on its own merit, there are serious inter-relationships between the rules, which should be observed by the reader.

It is important to note that the rules by themselves cannot work; they have to be applied and managed. Management is largely about behaviour, therefore if these rules are to yield positive results, the appropriate behaviour should be put behind them.

We expect that each business operator will apply his/her keen considerations to the peculiarity of the business such that operations may be optimized.

The Rules

RULE # 1: REGISTER YOUR BUSINESS BEFORE YOU START OPERATIONS.

It is required by law that all businesses whether profit or non-profit be registered with the Companies Office of Jamaica. If your business is not registered, it is not a business, legally speaking. In most situations you cannot open a business bank account or do business with utility companies or even rent/lease office space if you do not have a registered business or business name. In those cases where you are able to do business with just your personal name, you are running a risky situation.

In order to register your business, you may choose one of two means. Either you register your business name as a sole trader in which case, your status is that of a sole trader. As a mere business name, you will operate under the "Trading as" status, meaning that your business is not a limited liability company. The alternative is to register the business as a limited liability company. This second option is the better option because your liability in the business is limited to your investment in that business (you may still be personally liable under special tax legislations, however or in cases where you put up yourself as a guarantee for your business). If someone successfully sues the business, your personal assets may not be affected. If you are registered only as a business name, you could be sued by others and your personal assets such as your car and house could be exposed. It is difficult for a business to grow and be successful if it not formally registered as a limited liability company or a partnership with similar attributes.

The registration process is easy. You may choose to go to the Companies Office and with the guidance of officers at the Office, fill out the forms or you may ask your accountant or an attorney to have it done. If you choose to ask for professional assistance, be reminded that a fee will be incurred. In the case where you are registering a business with multiple owners, you may want to include special provisions in view of future possibilities regarding death, transfer of shares and other company matters. In such a situation, it may be a better idea to choose a professional, such as an attorney, to have the registration process done for you.

RULE # 2: KNOW THE KIND OF BUSINESS YOU ARE IN.

Let's say that you operate a bar, what kind of business are you in? If you are inclined to think that you are in the bar business or the liquor selling business, you would be short changing your vision of the business. In order to come to a clear understanding of the type of business you are in, start with this question; Why do people come to a bar?☐ I am certain you are now clearer as to the kind of business you are in. You now may want to think that you are in fact in the entertainment/hospitality business.

You may ask yourself, what is the purpose of being able to clearly define the business you are in? The answer to that is very simple. An understanding of the business you are in helps you to plan more astutely, more accurately and to identify the opportunities and threats existing in that sector to which your business belongs.

The fact that bars are for entertainment, brings with it the necessity to install big screen TVs, pool tables and facilitate karaoke singing. The expansion of your regular bar service to include these other forms of entertainment increases revenue and profitability. All major pubs in England have big screen TV because the pub is where a lot of football and cricket fans watch matches. We have adopted the model in Jamaica in the form of Sports Bars. This speaks volumes about how much more we now understand our businesses. We now have sports bars all over the place. There is also a need to find food for people who are spending so much time drinking and watching TV. This now necessitates having a restaurant as an addition to a bar; sports bars in particular. Every sports bar has an eatery and as such, this has become a major source of income for the operators of these establishments.

The videographer who records weddings, rarely realizes that he/she is in the entertainment and filming business. Watching a wedding on television is a form of entertainment, as much as it is a form of filmmaking. Videographers are also media personnel. The ordinary video man can, therefore, graduate to becoming a movie producer or film director if he/she carries such aspirations. It, therefore, pays for him/her to see this vision from early in the game.

What of restaurants? Many restaurateurs think they are in the food business. The food business is a part of other types of business; a segment in an industry. People must eat; food, therefore, it is a necessity like health care and education. However, food is one of the largest parts of the entertainment and hospitality industries. If you are operating a successful restaurant you should therefore open your eyes to the possibility that one day you could open a hotel, a casino or even a small school for the culinary arts. The business of catering to events is also just around the corner.

Understanding the business that you are in will help you to spot opportunities and to plan strategically to grasp these opportunities at the appropriate times. It is, therefore, imperative that you know what kind of business you are in. In your quest to better understand this rule, you may now want to contemplate the following questions;

> a.   What kind of businesses are the barbers, taxi operators, dressmakers and the motor vehicle mechanics in?
>
> b.   Based on where you are in your business, what other business ventures do you think you can successfully take on?
>
> c.   How do you want to expand the business, backward or forward?

Careful consideration of the forgoing questions should put you on a path of growth and expansion possibilities for your business.

> RULE # 3: WHEN PLANNING YOUR BUSINESS, ALWAYS SET REASONABLE FINANCIAL GOALS AND OBJECTIVES.

What do you think is meant by this? In designing your business plan, you have to ask yourself specific questions as to what you want the business to achieve in the near future and in the long term. What level of sales do you think you can achieve and how is this justified? What is the target profit? What are the targeted levels of expenditure? What are the sources of capital available to your business and what are the costs?

Every time you plan to achieve a target level of revenue you have to back this up with a target level of expenditure, depending on how much you want your asset and sales to grow. If you are planning to eliminate debt that was previously incurred, this must also be a part of your business planning. All aspects of the business must be well calculated and catered to.

Some small business operators think that they should not put a limit on how much the business earns or on the level of projected profits. This could be a fatal error. The fact is that your earnings are always largely a function of what you spend. If your earning ambitions are too high, you may find yourself spending too much to meet those ambitions and this may exceed the spending capacity of the business and crippling debt may be introduced into the business.

Let me give you an example. Let us assume that you are operating a bakery that sells bread and other baked products. In the event that you want to sell more bread, you may have to expand the capacity of your bakery by purchasing more machinery, expanding the physical plant and increasing the pool of personal. All of this may come with heavy financial burden in the short term and could cripple the business even in the face of potential increases in sales and profitability. You must therefore plan with clearly calculated financial objectives. When Hitler was planning to conquer Europe and the world, he never thought much about the significant cost of his expansion. Subsequently he made a significant loss on the war.

Your financial goals must spell out, in specific terms, what you want the business to achieve and in what time frame. Let us look at two typical financial objectives;

1. To make a net profit of $300,000 within the first six months of operation.

2. To earn gross revenues of $3,000,000 in the first six months of operation.

When you combine these two financial objectives what you get is a plan that says that you hope to make a net profit of $300,000 (10%), on total revenues of $3,000,000 in the first six months of operation.

Other financial objectives may cover things such as investment, capital budgeting, debt, equity financing and expansion. What level of debt can you sustain? What proportion of the total assets do you want the debt to be (leveraging)? How do you propose to acquire the funding for the business? What time frame are you setting to make a profit and what is the rationale for that? All these are legitimate questions in pursuit of well-defined business objectives. Prior to making any financial objectives, you must be aware of the likely consequences of these on the business. Every benefit that your business will have, comes with a cost. It is an unavoidable fact that cost is a function of the pursuit of revenues and profits. Cost is therefore a constant item in the consideration for business.

Many business operators make the dreaded mistake of setting their plans based on their personal objectives. Take for example if your main aim is to build a 12 bedroom house for your family of three. You try to figure out how quickly the business can provide you with the cash to start the foundation. This kind of financial attitude is suicidal and quite frankly, we have seen many businesses die from it. The revenue from the business should not be used to impress your neighbours or your wife; it is to be ploughed back into the businesses. You should therefore only include your salary in the business plan and not the dream house that you want to build. Very simply put, business objectives are for business plans and should not be confused with personal objectives in a manner that threatens the success or survival of the business.

RULE # 4: NEVER GO INTO BUSINESS OR CHANGE YOUR BUSINESS OPERATION IN ANY WAY, WITHOUT A WELL THOUGHT BUSINESS PLAN.

Your business plan is the blueprint for your business operation. This is what you should depend on for guidance and management of the business.

Let us go into a little statistics. In a broadcast on CNN some time ago, it was stated that over ninety percent of the small businesses that fail in the USA were set up by persons who had no training in business management. It is a similar case in Jamaica. Every day, you have a dressmaker, a tailor, a bar owner, a restaurateur, et al, starting up businesses. However, when you investigate the backgrounds of these people, there is no record of them being trained in business management. Business management is always a gut feeling thing for many of them. They see, what they think is a need and jump into business to satisfy that perceived need. Sometimes the need for a service or product is not economically viable, but these people may never know that, hence the business fails. That is, however, not the only reason for start-up failures.

Every serious business endeavour should start with a business plan. The plan is your blueprint for building that business. Without it, you are gliding in the dark and without much to guide you to the correct destination. We have recognized that developing a business plan is not the easiest thing to do. It is an area of expertise that requires a well-trained mind; by way of education, experience and best practice.

The business plan must have at its core, a well-designed marketing plan which itself must be arrived at by careful assessment of the industry in which you plan to operate. All fundamental issues must be well researched and systematically developed in order to have a cohesive plan that connects all aspects of the business; finance, marketing, and operation. Any business plan that is lacking in these elements along with the respective cohesive interconnectivity is likely to fail.

Sometimes the business plan is not about a new venture, it may be something of a going concern or even an expansion.

If you are going to do such things as expand the business or buy another business and these were not in the originally business plan, the plan ought to be modified to include these new ideas. In addition, both the marketing and the financial plans must be adjusted for overall consistency and practical cohesiveness. As indicated before, many businesses fail because the owners attempt to modify the business without a plan. In the past, some businesses were able to survive such unplanned moves. Nowadays, however, in the very competitive environment, such sins do not go unpunished. The risks are far too great, planning therefore, is a requirement.

More on business planning can be found in the comprehensive text on **How to Develop a Successful Business Plan.**

RULE # 5: DO NOT BORROW MONEY WHEN YOU NEED IT.

We know that this rule may sound strange to you. One of the authors of this book usually gets a surprised look from students in the class whenever the rule was laid down. Usually, it was met with almost unanimous disapproval from the over 70 students in the class. Nonetheless, the rule is a very powerful one and should be observed by everybody and we mean everybody in business. To fully explain the rule let us go back to a battlefield example.

> *If you try to negotiate peace after your army has been captured, you will be negotiating from a position of weakness. This you should never be allowed to happen.*

A business owner walks into a banker's office dejected man. Today he has some big bills to pay. The bills are overdue and he badly needs a loan to cover them. He, therefore, makes a passionate request to the banker. The manager sets some tough conditions for the loan and these conditions include putting up his house as collateral.

This business owner now finds himself in a financially precarious position and with little room to maneuver. Had he gone for the loan well in advance of the time it was needed, he would be in a better position to negotiate the conditions of the loan. The house as collateral may not even have been considered. You should not wait until you need cash to seek it. The fact is that when your business is strong and doing well, banks favour you and you get the best deals. When your business is in a financial bind you may not be welcomed. Of course this depends on your customer history with the bank. However, at this point, your business will be considered a risk and conditions will be put in place to offset the risks.

You may want to ask the question, "How will you know that you will need the money two, four or even twelve months away?" Planning makes this easy. Proper business planning allows you to foresee things such as the financial needs of the business. Surely you will not foresee everything; however, a good business plan will provide a strong and reliable indicator as to what the future needs of the business will be. The practice of recording and budgeting allows you to plan and forecast the future with usable accuracy.

Table 1-1 is an example of a simple cash forecast. Total outflows for the quarter exceeds total inflows by $77,084. Such a forecast will signal to the manager that something must be done to offset the future shortfall. In a case where the shortfall is inevitable, funding must be sought to ensure that cash is on hand. If a loan is the best option, arrangement for this must be made from the start of the period and NOT at the exact time the cash is required. In the example, the interest rate was projected at 15% with a 12 month repayment period. These are two key factors that must be considered in cash budgeting, because variations on these amounts can affect the cash budget one way of the other.

	Cash Budget Jan. 1 - Mar. 31			
	1st. Qrt.	Jan.	Feb.	Apr.
Opening Balance	100000	100000	350972	186944
Revenue	1400000	400000	500000	500000
Loan	600000	600000		
Total Inflows	2100000	1100000	850972	686944
Outflow:				
Purchases	1400000	500000	400000	500000
Utilities	145000	45000	50000	50000
Salaries and Wages	360000	120000	120000	120000
Loan Repayment	162084	54028	54028	54028
Other expenses	110000	30000	40000	40000
Total Outflows	2177084	749028	664028	764028
Net Cash Flows	-77084	350972	186944	-77084

Table 1-1— Mini Cash Forecast

One of the fundamental aspects of a good financial/business plan is the contingencies that go with it. Does your business plan have contingencies built into it? In a business where sales are affected by seasonality, the magnitude of the effects may not be easily determinable. This can create irreversible financial problems for your business. If you know this, you can take steps to prevent a business catastrophe by making financial arrangements prior to the time of need.

Always remember, that the prevention of financial problems lies in good planning, timely decision-making and financial pragmatism. You may have a good plan, make excellent decisions but if you procrastinate, the business may still be doomed.

People have made solid plans to go to heaven long before they die. You should, therefore, be able to plan your business for a few years of success.

RULE # 6: GET TO KNOW A BUSINESS WELL BEFORE YOU INVEST IN IT.

The depth to which you carry this rule will depend on your investment perspective. If you are investing in stocks and shares on the Jamaican Stock Exchange, the level of knowledge that is required would be different if you were actually buying a business. When you own a business you need to know as much as you can about the business. This will allow you to make decisions and to assist at the operational, should become necessary.

The majority of the small businesses in this country are operated by one or two persons. This says something about the need for you to fully understand the business operations. If the human resource in the business is inadequate (under-staffed), each person has to do more in order for the business to survive.

Another key reason you should observe this rule is that, as the business grows you would have had enough time to learn the business and this will allow you to grow with the business.

In the case where you are just an investor, your knowledge of the business should expand to the industry in which the business operates. Instead of just understanding his wife, a man should try to understand women and the socio-cultural environment in which they live. You should know about those factors that affect the business one way or the other. Here we are talking about government regulations, competitors' action, technology, etc. When you understand the business and the environment in which it operates, you can predict how the environmental factor will affect the business. Ultimately, this will enable you to make a reasonable judgment on the wisdom of your investment.

RULE # 7: BANK MANAGERS ARE NOT THE OWNERS OF YOUR BUSINESS; DO NOT LET THEM DICTATE TERMS TO YOU.

Simply put, do not allow the banks more say than is necessary. Most times when a bank finds a weakness in your negotiating position it will exploit it. Currently, there is evidence to suggest that the profits of banks relate directly in some ways to the ignorance of many of their customers. The banks cannot be blamed in all cases, however, because caveat emptor (let the buyer beware) is still relevant.

Let us look again at the case of trying to get a loan from the bank. Some loan officers like to tell you what type of loan to take and over what period you can best manage the repayment. If you are going to apply for a loan and you do not know the period for which you will need the loan, then why are you applying for the loan? It is like going to the doctor but not being able to tell the doctor where you are feeling the pain.

Another issue is that of collateral. Banks like to tell you what kind of collateral they would like to have. If you have multiple collaterals that are suitable, do not give the best one to the bank. For the longest while, banks have insisted that they do not lend money on the strength of collaterals, but more so, on the ability of the borrower to repay. If this principle is true of the modus operandi of banks, managers should have no problem accepting any suitable collateral from you, once your business qualifies for the loan.

Another area in which banks sometimes behave dictatorially, concerns the disbursement of funds to your business. Sometimes the poor disbursements of funds can be more harmful than no loan at all. Take the case of an emergency medical operation in which the patient has little time to spare. Whatever treatment is necessary at the prescribed moment must be provided right away, otherwise, the situation could get worse. While your business suffers from the lack of capital, some bank managers dictate a disbursement schedule that runs contrary to the needs of the business.

With good cash budgeting and planning, you will be clear as to cash flow needs. The cash flow needs should be the main indicator of loan disbursement needs. The bank will be helpful only if the appropriate schedule is in place. If the proposed schedule is counterproductive to that required, you will need to point this out to the bank and to convince the manager otherwise.

By all accounts, you should know your business better than your banker. If this is not the case something is terribly wrong. We will forever maintain that business owners should be careful in taking advice from their bankers.

You can sit and discuss the problems or fortunes of your business but never allow the bank manager to dictate lending terms to you. Always remember, the more money you borrow the more the bank earns from you. This interest that you will have to pay must come from the revenue of the business. Since this has the effect of increasing your expenses, it means that your profit will suffer or your losses will increase. You must always be mindful of any suggestion that seeks to increase your overall interest charges thus adversely affecting your profitability. When profitability is affected growth will be affected.

On the matter of savings and investments in things such as fixed deposits, you should have the last word. In Jamaica, people have a tradition of asking bank managers what they should do with their money. People should ask the banks about their services and products. After getting this information, they should then decide what they want to do with their money. A friendly bank manager should not be taken as a substitute for educating yourself on matters of personal and business finance. This will allow you to make independent financial decisions about your business.

RULE # 8: YOUR BUSINESS MAY NEED 3 - 6 MONTHS OF PRECAUTIONARY FUNDS IF IT IS TO SURVIVE IN THE CHALLENGING START-UP PERIOD.

Whether you are a first-time parent or a seasoned one, the birth of your child may see you out of a job for at least a short time. While being out of a job, you will still have to provide for yourself and the baby and possibly the entire household. Where will the money come from to provide for the needs of the household including the baby? These would have to come from money that was saved for this kind of possibility. Similarly with a business, the startup of operations will have to be catered to by working capital that is already in place. It cannot be that you are depending wholly on income from daily sales. Depending on the nature of the business, this may be a very foolish thing to do.

You will have payroll, transportation, utilities, promotional expenses and purchases to deal with. These expenses cannot wait on the possibility of sales income because that may never be realized in the first few weeks or even the first few months of operation. A business, therefore, needs what is called precautionary funds to carry it for a period, in the case enough income is not earned within the period right after startup. If you are running a restaurant, chances are you may see some sales the very first day of operation. However, the first two week sales may not be enough for you to cover your cash needs for the business. It may not even be enough to cover your staff salaries in the first two weeks. You do not want to open the restaurant in the morning and be in your office praying for customers to buy breakfast so that you can get money to buy chicken to make lunch. You should not be waiting on sales in order to pay your grocery suppliers or to pay your electricity bills. That is not how you should conduct your new business venture.

If you start the business with a loan, chances are you will have to start paying back the loan at the end of the first month, unless you have a moratorium in place from the lending institution. If ever you are to default on your loan payment, it should not be on the first month. While I am not saying you should not try to pay your first month's obligation from your sales income, I am imploring you to not depend on sales to deal with all your early working capital obligations. Ensure that you have working capital in place to carry on the business for 3 to 6 months, if sales fail to measure up during that initial period of operation. Like we indicated earlier, the gestation period will depend on the nature of the business. A restaurant at an excellent location will have a shorter 'gestation' period than a stationary business in a less than ideal location or a farming operation for tree crops. The assessment must be made on the basis of the rate of acceleration of sales in the business.

Let us look at a less popular business for a change; a medical practice such as a general practitioner's office or that of a dentist. We have seen these kinds of businesses set up without much consideration for a long learning curve. The fact that some of these kinds of businesses do not advertise, it sometimes will take a long time before potential patients know that they are there or that you are a worthy medical doctor. In many cases, like with other sectors and industries, you will be luring people away from other businesses so you will need time and you must start with enough fuel to go the distance before you can run on your own income.

In a more extreme case, an agricultural operation will take a longer period. The earliest that you can expect for a cash crop operation is about 3 - 6 months for cash crops. If you are into coffee, you will have to carry the burden for up to three years and if you are into poultry or rabbit you could be looking at 6 weeks to 4 months. Although poultry will take 6 - 8 weeks to be ready, the period between startup (preparation of the facility) and the marketing of the processed meat and up to collection of the income, could take up to six months. These examples go to show the level of meticulous planning and due diligence that should go into the setting up and running of a business. It is the neglect of aspects of these operations that may lead to failure of businesses that are otherwise potentially successful.

Sometimes we only need to apply a bit of clinical treatment to planned operations in order to avoid failure. It is part of having full knowledge of what you are getting involved with before you start. Sometimes you just have to spend time dotting the "Is" just to ensure that the paragraphs in that chapter of the business is well constructed.

RULE # 9: THOROUGHLY INVESTIGATE THE SERVICES THAT FINANCIAL INSTITUTIONS OFFER BEFORE BECOMING A CUSTOMER.

To become a customer of a bank means a number of things. As a customer, you entrust the bank with your money, you borrow money from the bank and you also avail yourself of one or more of the many services the bank offers. Those are enough reasons to research financial institutions before you start doing business with them. Here we are talking about not only banks but credit unions, insurance companies, building societies, loan companies, etc.

When you deposit cash at the banks or in building societies, you are technically lending money to these institutions. Have you ever asked yourself how it is possible for the banks to pay interest on savings? The money that is deposited at banks is lent out to other customers who have to pay interest on these loans. The interest paid on loans are higher than the interest paid to you the depositor or saver, which therefore makes it possible for the banks to pay you interest on your savings. Now, if when your friends ask you for a loan, you tell them to borrow it from your bank, it would be a better alternative for all concerned.

While you are trying to decide whether the interest rate is acceptable, you should also take a look at the quality of the service offered by the bank. You should know the loan policy of the financial institution. If you find these policies unsuitable, you should go to another institution that is able to offer you a better deal. No financial institution that is not customer friendly is worthy of your business.

Since your business will need a wide range of financial services as it grows, you must ensure that the financial institution of your choice is able to offer at least most of those services. Here we are talking about, deposits, chequing accounts, money transfer, standing orders, FX accounts, overdrafts facility, letters of credit, loans and mortgages, bank guarantees, internet banking, ATM services, payroll services, etc. It is important to know about these banking services and their associated costs. This kind of information is required from day one and since most banks have a schedule of these services and the associated fees, it should be of no problem to get up to date with these services.

Let us delve into a little more detail. Banks are now charging for everything, from opening an account to the encashment of cheques. These are two services that were previous free. We were under the impression that certain overheads and small tasks were covered by the interest that the banks earn on savings, alas! That seems to have changed drastically over the past 20 years. A massive revolution took place in the financial sector in the mid-90s. All commercial banks now have a schedule of service fees. At the time of writing one of these two authors looked at one of these schedules. The list was so long, it reads like a price list at a supermarket. You need to know these fees because these can add up to large amounts and can adversely affect your cash flow at the end of the month. Most if not all of the fees attracts GCT which means additional cash outflows.

Most institution charges a commitment fee to process the loans that you seek. This fee is usually stated as a percentage of the loan amount. If the commitment fee is 1% of the loan being applied for, a loan of $2M would attract a commitment fee will be $20,000 (2,000,000 x 0.01). You will now have to add other fixed fees to that and before you know it; you are in a serious crisis.

Research your bank carefully while searching for alternative and cheaper sources of doing business. If you are having problems getting the information, speak frankly with a representative of the bank or better, consult with an independent small business expert if you think you need that kind of support. Although that kind of consultation has a cost it may be a way of saving on other form of expenses or even to boost profitability through revenue increase or cost savings.

> RULE # 10: IF YOU ARE TAKING A LOAN OR DEPOSITING FUNDS, ALWAYS MAKE SURE THAT INTEREST AND INTEREST RATE ARE FULLY EXPLAINED TO YOU BY THE FINANCIAL ENTITY.

This is something that has always eluded the proper working relationship between banks and their customers. A number of law suits involving allegations of overcharging by banks that have be won by customers. In our line of duty as business consultants we have discovered many persons who do not understand the concept of interest or interest rate. Some who understand the concept do not understand how it is calculated. We speak from a position of firsthand knowledge because we have had to write business plans for a number of individuals and businesses. One of the things that we normally do for our clients is to explain the interest and interest rates that will be incurred by the businesses, for the loans that they seek. It is appalling that some banks did not see it proper to do this for their customers.

In recent years and since the advent of the Fair Trading Commission, actions have been taken to address the problem. There was a time when a large number of bank customers had no idea how interest was calculated. It goes to emphasize that since banks do not look out for you, you have to look out for yourself.

When an interest rate is quoted to you there are a number of important questions that you should put to the banker. What is the effective rate of interest? Will the interest rate vary over time? Is there a late payment penalty (most times there is)? Is the interest calculated on the balance of the loan/deposit or is a fixed amount for the life of the loan/deposit? If a banker tells you that your loan will incur compound interest, you know you are unto something very risky. If the loan interest is calculated on the reducing balance, it means the more of the principal that you pay off, the less interest you pay. If the interest is calculated as a fixed interest, it would be an expensive interest for the business but the interest would be constant. What is the importance of knowing about the interest and the interest rates?

When you take a loan, the main expense item for that loan is the interest. You may incur various fees in acquiring the loan, however; the interest will stand as the main item of expense for that loan. In instances where you default, penalty will come into the picture and this too is an expense. In order to explain the rule further, let us look at a few of the interest mathematics.

If a banker quotes you an interest of 18% on a fixed interest/add-on loan of $500,000 for 5 years, the actual rate that you pay comes out to almost 36%. This is however, not easy for the untrained business manager to see. What you will see is 5 years interest which amounts to $450,000 (18% x $500,000 x 5 years). This is then added to the loan (principal) of $500,000, and then divided by 60 months (the loan period) to get the monthly payment of $15,833.33. However, even after you have made the first 24 months payment, you will still be paying interest calculated on the original principal. The direct alternative to this is the reducing balance loan. Let us see how that one works.

The reducing balance loan is very popular these days. If you borrow the same half a million as in the example above, at the same interest rate, your first-month interest payment will be $7,500. That is {($500,000 x 18%)} / 12, plus the portion of the principal that is due. The full monthly payment is usually worked out as an amortization by the financial institution. This will be about $12,696. Total interest on this loan for 5 years would be $261,802 while the interest on the fixed interest loan would be $450,000. It should now be clear which loan is cheaper and why it is important for a businessman to understand what the bank is doing. If you do not understand the mechanics of the loan it could drive you crazy.

I am aware that not all business owners are up to date on these mathematical calculations. If you are one such businessman, you will need to have someone in your corner, an accountant or someone on the managerial team that is au fait with these financial dimensions. The interest rate is one of the main means by which financial institutions make money and they pay keen attention to it. You, therefore, must pay keen attention to it because it is an expense for you and, therefore, a burden on profit.

RULE # 11: THE FUNCTIONAL RELATIONSHIP BETWEEN FINANCE AND MARKETING SHOULD NEVER BE NEGLECTED OR MISUNDERSTOOD.

It is over a long period that a keen understanding of the functional relationship between finance and marketing to have been developed among small business operators. Some operators still do not understand it. In years gone by, some organizations treated marketing as an outcast and as a result, the business suffered in sales and profitability. Do you know the relationship between marketing and finance?

Okay, let us explain in one simple statement; marketing is the core of all business operation. It is around this core that everything else revolves. Since marketing has to do with supplying customer needs at a profit, it goes without much debate that the statement is true. If there is nothing to market, there will be no sale, regardless of what finance has in place initially. It is a chicken and egg situation For some persons, but for us marketing is core. With good marketing you can start a business without a cent; however, once you start collecting funds, once you are in receipt of revenue, you are now into the world of financial management. So how do we make the link?

In a business that has good growth potential marketing will determine what is called a market potential. This is the total amount that can be sold by the industry. Sale potential is what the business can sell in a particular period in the industry to which it belongs over a given period. Let us lock down the understanding on this. The market potential is usually bigger than the sales potential.

Assume that you are in a particular industry; say the auto parts industry that can sell 20 Billion for the year. You are about to start a small auto part business and after careful analysis, you forecast that you can sell $50 Million for the year, that is your sale potential. This sales forecast is what all the financial planning for the business will revolve around.

A number of assumptions would have been employed to arrive at this forecast. There will be a need for human resources (staffing), warehousing, advertising, stock purchases, etc. These factors of production will be determined by the estimates of what the business can sell for the period under consideration. Are you seeing where we are going now? All these inputs would have been as a direct result of the marketing sale forecast. This would then have to be translated into financial considerations and that is how financial plans get shaped by marketing plans. That right there is the connection between marketing and finance.

Recently when Apple wanted to increase its sales on the iPhone it looked to China. It then employed a powerful marketing team to conduct research and to come up with a plan. Even before that, the marketing team in conjunction with the technical team had to get the design of the phone in line with what the market demanded. In the end, Apple made the biggest profit in the history of any corporate body.

In the tourism sector, there are seasonal influences on the demand for the tourism product. If you are the operator of a small hotel and you have plans to expand the business (to add more rooms for example). You may want to plan your expansion in the off-season so that you can pick up the pieces during the high season while at the same time minimizing the adverse effects of construction. In this scenario, you may want to time the funding (loan or equity) with the market projections.

When banks or other lending institutions ask you to submit your business plan, one of the main things they look at are your sales projections. They want to see where the money is coming from to support your proposal for the repayment of the loan. Tt seems that some banks do not bother to look at the other parts of the business plan. We have seen a number of business plans in which the financial projections do not match the marketing plan. Yet loans were extended to the businesses. In this respect, we can now put it to you that a number of businesses that have failed because not enough attention was paid to the business plan. Had the attention been given, it would have been noticed that the different aspects of the plan are not in harmony. We must say to you without reservation that it is not the easiest thing to construct a workable business plan.

A business plan is based on many assumptions that must be clinically constructed. If the planner is out of sync with business reality the assumptions will be wrong and the projections will be flawed. This could lead to business failure to due poor planning.

Marketing is the core of all business operation, be it big or small. The earlier we recognize this fact, the better the start in our business endeavour.

RULE # 12: FRIENDSHIP AND MONEY CAN BE SERIOUS ENEMIES, BE CAREFUL HOW YOU MIX THEM.

If a friend comes to you and requests from your business, a loan of $300,000, how would you respond? Should this be an ordinary decision to lend some money to a friend or is it a business decision? Another question you could ask yourself is whether you think your friend will repay the money? What if the money is repaid much later than you expected or not repaid at all? In such a case the business could lose $300,000. Is this something you wish for your business? Certainly we hope that you do not respond in the affirmative.

It is only after this careful analysis that you begin to understand that you cannot just lend money from your business to a friend. It should be an investment decision like any other. As such, this decision should be subjected to careful analysis and assessment as you would do if you were about to buy shares on the stock market. As a matter of fact, this money could be used for other investments. Why then lend the money to your friend?

Now if your friend wants the money to start up a business you may go ahead and lend the money but there are a number of things that you have to do. The thing that you must consider is that you will need to reduce the risk of getting back your money. You also have to ensure that the business to be started by your friend will not hurt your business. So if he/she is proposing to set up a business similar to yours in the vicinity of your location, you would have to refuse the request.

On the other hand, if his use of the money is a proposed business venture you would have to evaluate this proposed business venture to see what risks are involved. This is a very reasonable approach because if the venture fails your money will be lost. There is also an opportunity to invest in a new business should you choose to. This will now become a serious investment decision rather than merely lending money to a friend.

As far as finance and prudent business management are concerned, any money coming out of the business other than that for normal expenses and profit sharing must be seen as a direct investment and should be treated accordingly. If your friend wishes you well he will also pay you interest on the money that is lent to them. Documents must be signed and the whole thing consummated as a business deal. If your friends object to this approach he/she does not deserve the money.

When you are lending money out of your personal account you can do whatever you choose. That is a personal financial decision. When it is a business decision you have to be very astute and take care of the business.

Remember, when the auditors come they will want to know where that withdrawal went and how it was handled.

RULE # 13: THE TYPE OF FUNDING THAT YOU SEEK FOR YOUR BUSINESS SHOULD MATCH THE INVESTMENT TYPE.

Many years ago we had a client who came to us to write a business plan. He had gone to the bank to seek a loan to purchase stock (inventory) for his business. The bank agreed to lend him the cash over a three year period but had asked him to submit a business plan. The loan would be on fixed interest for the period of three years. In those days, fixed interest loans were popular.

After we began gathering information for the plan we realized that he did not need a loan for three years. What he needed was short term financing to shore up working capital, in this case, his inventory. We recommended to him to get the money from the credit union and to pay it off within one year. We then proceeded to demonstrate to him how much he will save in interest on the loan.

This goes to show that there is a structured approach to loan management. Loans are not to be taken because it means a cash injection in the business. All loans come with a price and that price is what we call interest. When you take the wrong loan you may end up paying the higher price and stifling the business along the way.

Long term investments such as capital investments must be funded by long-term loans, if you are using loans. On the other hand, short-term investments such as building up inventory and paying a month's salary should be funded by short-term money. An add-on loan of $50,000 at an interest rate of 20% for three years will cost the business total interest of $30,000 over the loan period. By comparison, if you take the same size loan with monthly interest calculated on the balance you would pay far less interest and you could relieve yourself of the loan any time you want. If you attempt to pay out a long-term loan before the period is up you will incur an early payout penalty. Good financial management is about how you juggle your financial operation across the board.

Short-term loans must only be incurred if the projected cash flow shows that the business can comfortably handle the payment in the short term. Usually, a short-term loan may carry higher monthly payments and, therefore, the ability of the business to fulfill these higher payments will avoid default and protect the credit rating of the business. If the business can only handle lower payments, spread these payments over a longer period while ensuring that the loan is not used for long-term financial needs. The mismatch of funding type and investment has been a big problem for small businesses in this country; do not make that very common mistake.

RULE # 14: IN BUSINESS YOU SHOULD ASSIGN RESPONSIBILITIES BUT TRUST NO ONE.

This rule may feel a little drastic and unfriendly; you, however, have to look beyond personal feelings to understand what we are saying here. To get an even better appreciation of this rule, consider the effect on your business of a massive fraud and you will see our position on this very important matter.

Running a business is not merely how you feel about people, unless you are a Doctor or a Psychologist. It is about running a business, managing revenues, making profits minimizing cost and managing people. It is not that you should not allow people to run your business, you must, however, put systems and procedures in place to prevent people from draining your business of cash and kind.

Whether you go to business school or to the college of experience, the lesson is always about how to run a business not how to trust people. If you do not have a good system of control and you trust people to move your inventory, lodge your cash and collect your money then very soon your will be out of business and seeking charity assistance. The irony is that not even charitable organizations operate with just the trust of people. If this ever happens, everybody will be the poorer for it.

RULE # 15: DO NOT CONFUSE CASH WITH PROFIT.

Let us start with a very simple example. If you start a business today and you invest $200,000.00 in cash, at the end of the first day of trading, you find yourself with $50,000.00, generated by sales. Does this mean that you have $50,000.00 in profit? Certainly it does not mean that. Cash and profit are very different and should never be seen as the same thing. Many small business operators make the error of thinking that cash is and treating it as profit. While a detailed discussion of this difference is outside of the scope of this book we will nonetheless try to furnish a useful explanation on the difference between the two.

Cash is absolute money that is limited by its own value. Profit, on the other hand, is the excess of revenue over expenses over a stated actual or projected period. The interesting thing about profit is that even though it is denominated in monetary values (just like cash), it is more a paper value than anything else. When you say the business has $50,000.00 in cash you should be able to show that money, it is physically there, in your till or at the bank in deposits, cheques an savings. If your business, however, makes a profit of $1M over twelve months you most likely will not be able to show that profit in cash. That profit may be tied up in inventory, capital investments (such as building and machinery) and accruals. As a matter of fact, you may even have more cash than profit.

What does this understanding of the difference between cash and profit means to the small business operator? A large cash surplus in the bank account may be perceived as a sign of a good profit. Such a perception may lead to overspending in respect of profit taking and salary payments or withdrawals. This will most definitely endanger the survival of the business.

At the end of a financial year, you may find yourself with $250,000.00 in cash, yet you have incurred a loss of $70,000.00. What this simple means is that your revenues fell below your expenses. On the contrary, the business could be cashless but profitable.

Investment decisions must not be made only on the basis of cash in hand, but rather on the basis of both cash and profitability. The two factors of cash and profit are interdependent for the survival of the business. When the business is strapped for cash, investments cannot be made and if investments are not made cash revenues cannot be earned. The interplay with the two can be very tricky and will require astute financial management in order to get a good right balance.

Finally, we are not saying that cash is the only form of investment; however, without cash the business would be like a car trying to run without fuel, it is going nowhere.

> RULE # 16: RECORD KEEPING IS THE FOUNDATION OF BUSINESS INFORMATION AND IT IS ALSO A LEGAL REQUIREMENT. IT SHOULD BE PRACTICED BY ALL BUSINESSES AND IN ACCORDANCE WITH SET STANDARDS AND LEGISLATIVE CONSIDERATIONS.

The record keeping of the Greeks facilitated the development of the English language. Just the same, the circumnavigation of the African continent was facilitated by the great record keeping of those who had gone before. Record keeping documents the history of your business and gives a guide to the future. In the present, this can be used to explain your current situation and, therefore, suggests a path for the future. Prior to the advent of the General Consumption Tax, most operators of small businesses did not keep proper records of their business activities. If this is your practice you are setting up yourself for imminent disaster. Record keeping should not only be in existence in your business, it should be accurate and timely.

What records should you keep? This is a question for your accountant. We can, however, tell you that a cash book, inventory records, fixed asset register, a list of payables, a list of receivables, statement of financial status, income statement, production record, etc. In other words, you will need to have a full accounting system in place. We are not for one moment suggesting that you should have full competence in dealing with these records. What we are alluding to is that if you want to run a successful business these records should be in place. You will, therefore, need to have an accountant on board to drive this aspect of your operation. In order to foster a better appreciation of this rule let us outline briefly, the functions of each record.

> **The cash book:** This is a record that shows the transactions concerning cash payments and receipts. All cash transactions are recorded in the cash book. That includes cash movements in the bank account.

Inventory record: The inventory records pertain to your stock in trade (trading) or your raw materials (manufacturing). Stock going into or leaving storage, damaged stock and stock codes are all part of the inventory records.

Fixed Asset register: All the items of fixed asset that the business owns will be listed in this very important register. There will be a description of the asset, the quantity, a code, the date of purchase and a book value of the asset.

Payables: The accounts payable is a list of all the individuals and organizations that the business owes money. This excludes direct loans.

Receivables: This is a list of all the individuals and organizations that owe your business money.

Income Statement: This is the statement of your profit or loss performance over a specified period; monthly, quarterly or yearly. This is very important because it is the statement of ultimate performance of the business and also, it is one of the prime records from which your tax liability is calculated.

Statement of Financial position/Balance Sheet: This is a statement that sets out your assets and liabilities as at a given date. It allows you to calculate your net worth (i.e. the difference between your asset and your liabilities). If your liabilities exceed your assets, the business is in financial trouble and could become bankrupt. On the other hand, if the assets exceed the liabilities the business is solvent. I must point out here that not in all cases when liabilities exceed assets it means that the business is bankrupt. If the capital base is substantive enough it could soften the effects.

Normally you would start the business with an opening statement of financial position (balance sheet) and generate at least one per year. As time goes by you would be in a position to make comparisons, which will tell you the direction in which the business is going. Business growth is normally reflected on your balance sheet.

Production records: In a manufacturing concern, these records provide information on such things as production quantities, scheduling and production cost. One of the purposes of these records is to assist you in ascertaining production cost that will ultimately be used in pricing and other decision-making processes.

There are other records that must be considered. However, you should consult with your accountant, to put in place an accounting system that will work for you. Having an accountant working for you does not exonerate you, the Manager/Owner from having a working knowledge of your accounting system. If you plan to computerize your business, for heaven's sake, get computer literate.

Some other records that must be kept on hand include negotiations, customer complaints, supplier prices and correspondence, competitors' profiles, business contracts and any information relevant to the business. Records are more important than a good manager.

RULE # 17: IF YOU HAVE TO TAKE A LOAN, ALWAYS EXPLORE ALTERNATIVES BEFORE DECIDING WHERE TO BORROW MONEY.

Taking a loan for your business can lead to eternal hell for the business as well as it could help the business to get a life. A loan from any lending source is not revenue; it is a debt, a liability and should be avoided in the first place.

Prior to taking a loan, you must establish beyond doubt that the business needs that type of financing. You must also ensure that a loan is the most suitable option of raising the needed cash at the time.

Some of our colleagues think that we are anti-loans. Probably we are, but is there anything wrong with not wanting to take a loan? Taking a loan can be a good thing for your business; unfortunately loans favour businesses that do not need it. Simply put, when a loan goes bad, a big business with cash can recover; a small business, on the other hand, will die or be taken over by a big business. What about equity financing? Sometimes it is better to relinquish a portion of the ownership of the business in order to ensure its survival. As a matter of fact, the experiences of many past businesses reaffirm the adage, "want all lose all". If the prospects are good there are many persons who will be interested in purchasing a piece of your business.

The source of the loan could mean the difference between the loan being helpful and not. Many small businesses run to a commercial bank when all they need to do is to approach a development agency or a private venture capitalist. Will it be a credit union, a building society, an insurance company or a PC bank?

You have to know the available sources of funding in the country and decide which you would use in an eventuality. The knowledge as to where you can access funding should be acquired before you go into business. When a shuttle is to be sent to space literally over a million things can go wrong. The NASA people know and plan for this well ahead of the launch. That is probably one of the reasons business managers with a strong scientific background are successful.

Before you run to borrow money you should evaluate the alternatives and make a decision based on the following criteria;

    a. The terms and conditions of the loan.
    b. The turnaround time.
    c. The overall reputation of the lending organization.
    d. The accompanying services that the organization provides (after loan service).
    e. The interest rate (cost of the loan). This is the most important criterion for evaluating a lending source. The cost of a loan sometimes extends beyond the interest and interest rate.
    f. The loan default policy. How supportive is the lending institution in the event that you fall on bad times?

Although these criteria are not exhaustive, they are the most important you would consider before making a choice.

The whole thing can be traced to planning. If you plan your business properly you would know where you can get capital for your business if you need it. This is something that should be in your contingency plans.

Let us take you back to the issue of the cost of a loan. As pointed out earlier, there are other costs that are involved in the acquisition of a loan. These include processing fee, commitment fees, application fee and other charges. Sometimes these charges are indexed to the size of the loan. For instance, if a commitment fee of 2% is applicable to a loan, for every $100,000.00 in loan that you take you would have to pay $2,000.00 to the lending institution. You have to ensure that you know about these charges before making any commitment. This will also put you in a better position to compare the sources.

Over the past fifteen years, a plethora of micro lenders has sprung up over the country. Some of them are what we call loan sharks and must be avoided, because the cost of the loans provided by these institutions is high. If you have to use one of these lenders make sure you pay back in a short period because a long period will see you incurring a high interest cost. There is one good sign, however, the interest rates from these micro-finance lenders have come down over the years, due to stiff competition.

RULE # 18: CHOOSE CAREFULLY YOUR LOCATION BECAUSE THIS CAN IMPACT HEAVILY ON YOUR REVENUES.

I have included location as an item in the set of rules because it is as important to finance as it is to marketing. Poor location is already poor marketing and this will lead to low revenues and low profitability or even non-viability. There are many examples of improved locations, changing the fortunes of businesses for the better. The converse on that is also true.

A good business in a bad location is bad business. A good location is one that provides convenience for both the seller and the buyer. The location that you choose must be socially, legally and environmentally acceptable and must be suitable for your employees, customers and suppliers. If your business depends on pedestrian traffic in should be located in an area of high pedestrian density, such as city centers and towns. If it depends mainly on vehicular traffic, a two-way street with adequate parking is suitable, plus proper entrance to and from the location is desirable. Time of day, occasion and type of product must all be used to evaluate the location and to eventually choose which is appropriate for the business.

The choice of a good location does not stop with the current situation, it goes well into the future and therefore what prevails today may change in the next few years.

Over the past 20 years, traffic changes in the Kingston Metro regions have significantly modified the movement of pedestrian and traffic. Many have become one-way streets and many businesses have suffered as a direct result. In choosing a permanent location for your business, the future must be considered. This can be done with a bit of research to know whether the government has any plans for future development that may directly adversely affect your business. The issue of business location is a structural one and must never be overlooked.

RULE # 19: AVOID YOUR EMOTION WHEN MAKING BUSINESS DECISIONS.

One of the worse factors affecting businesses in this country is emotional decision making. You refused to implement a good idea because it was given to you by an employee, whom you do not like. You refused to pay the loan because you are upset with the bank. Instead of closing down the business, you continue to operate it at a loss because you love the business so much; there is great sentimental attachment. The fact is, while some business owners love their businesses the businesses do not love them. Some owners love their businesses to death.

Business decision making is in its own right a science. It requires a special ability that not everybody has. Business decisions should be made on the basis of thorough analysis of business information, actual and projected. There are times when it is less expensive to close down a business than to try to save it with a loan. When a business passes its critical point of viability, it is time to let it go. The same goes for a product that is no longer profitable; you need to remove it from your line unless you see where its continued inclusion in the inventory can increase the overall profitability of the business as in the case of loss leaders.

If you have to close a business that you have built over the last twenty years it can be a very emotional thing, massive hurt. That should not, however, deter you from doing what is right. The same kind of situation exists when a family member is not performing well and you may have to ask the person to leave your business. The fact is that those decisions have to be taken from time to time. We know that this is easier said than done. We also know that there are things that can be done to minimise the negative effects of those kinds of decisions. Whatever the problem, if you cannot handle it, then you may need to summon professional help.

On the matter of loans, many mistakes have been made as a direct result of emotion. Take the case of the businessman who took an expensive loan from a bank, just because the bank manager was a school friend of his. It is possible that the same loan could have been obtained from an alternative source at a more favourable interest rate. By way of the old school connection, the collateral requirement was relaxed and no business plan was required or the one submitted was not properly scrutinized. Eight months later and the loan goes bad, the bank seizes the realizable assets and the business goes under. Both the bank manager and the business man were terribly wrong in their dealings.

Forget about the friendship, business is business. As a businessman, your job is not to seek the quickest loan because someone may be your friend. Your job is to prevent the business from needing a loan. We are not saying that you cannot take a loan; however, you should guide the business in such a manner that it does not need a loan. Any lending institution that does not require a business plan for a business loan, especially start-up loan, is operating in a very questionable manner, be careful.

The fact that you may not be making emotional decisions about your business does not mean others may not make such decisions against you or your business. Since one of the toughest decisions to make is to close down the business, always remember this; do not allow a dying business to bring you down with it. The necropolis of unsuccessful businesses is not for you, give it up and start something new.

RULE # 20: DO NOT PAY BILLS BEFORE THEY ARE DUE, HOWEVER, PAY ON TIME.

Depending on which side of the fence you sit, you may or may not agree with us. There is no reason you should try to go to heaven if Jesus is not ready for you. When you pay your bills before they become due what are you trying to achieve, 110% credit rating? An excellent credit rating will do. It is just not prudent financial management to pay bills that are not due.

Take for instance that you have a bill of $200,000.00 to pay to one of your suppliers. If this cash that is now sitting in an account earning interest at 1% per month, is paid out two weeks ahead of due date you would have lost $1000 in interest. This amount could purchase fuel for a few deliveries.

Another thing about early payouts is that the cash you paid out too early could be (apart from an interest bearing account) invested in increasing inventory and, therefore, sales and profit. The money you pay to another company or individual is now available to them to do what you did not do with it. It represents an opportunity lost. The fact is if you pay too early it puts the creditor at a distinct advantage and you at a distinct disadvantage. Please run the business by the rules.

RULE # 21: ALWAYS PAY ATTENTION TO YOUR NET WORTH.

What is net worth? This is the difference between your liability and your assets. In other words, the difference between what you own and what you owe. If your liabilities exceed your assets you are in big trouble. It would mean that you are insolvent.

Let us further explain this concept. When you are insolvent and if you sell all your assets you would still not be able to cover all your liabilities. In such a case your net worth is negative. On the other hand, if your assets exceed your liabilities and you sell your assets, you would be able to cover your total liabilities.

This means that you would have a positive net worth and, therefore, your business will be solvent. One of the main aims of businesses is to widen the gap between asset and liabilities in a positive way. That is one very important way you will achieve good value for your business if you want to sell it.

While some of our colleagues in finance will say that profit is your bottom line, we will say that your bottom line is your net worth. No lending institution wants to lend money to a business that has a negative net worth. On this side of the coin, a business could get funding even when it is making a loss. Agri-businesses and some other businesses such as a winery can exist in losses for a number of years. Let us explain the different between profit and net worth so as to provide a clearer view of the rule.

Profit is what is left after all expenses have been accounted for and subtracted from income. Net worth is what is left after you have subtracted the total of your liabilities from the total of your assets. When a business is unprofitable for a period, it can still carry on because it could still have cash to continue its operation or it could borrow short-term funds. However, when a business has a negative net worth, which means that it liabilities exceed its assets, it is bankrupt.

When a business gets to this stage financially, it will need a capital injection in the form of equity.

No business will exist for too long with a growing negative net worth. A business must always look after its net worth. When a business has too high a debt relative to its equity base (debt ratio), it is over-leveraged. Leveraging your business can be advantageous. However, you should be careful not to incur too much debt.

Technically speaking, when a business has a negative networth it does not exist. It is now only a virtual business. Do you remember that the Eagle Financial Empire was sold for one "degay degay" dollar? One of the sad developments that we have noticed happening for as long as we have been involved in business management, is the fact that some of the owners of the businesses are the ones responsible for the erosion of net worth in their businesses. How does this happen? There are a number of ways.

 a. Owners take too high a salary.
 b. The growth of the business is not properly managed.
 c. Very poor cash management.
 d. Very little planning, especially long term planning.
 e. Owners do not keep proper records and are therefore not in a position to

analyze the business activity and therefore not able to make informed decisions.

When we talk about the richest men and women in the world, the figures are based on Net worth, not cash worth. True wealth is reflected in net worth. Many persons in Jamaica do not seem to understand that. The true indicator of growth in a business is not profit worth but net worth. We are not losing sight of the fact, however, that profit is the number one propellant for the growth of net worth. Whatever you do, watch your net worth. Net worth can also be increased by the growth in value of business assets and that should be one of the push of your financial discipline.

> RULE # 22: DO NOT BUY PUSS IN A BAG. IF YOU PLAN TO BUY A BUSINESS MAKE SURE THAT YOU KNOW WHAT YOU ARE BUYING BEFORE YOU CLOSE THE DEAL.

This rule comes without sympathy or forgiveness. There are times when investors prefer the option of buying an existing business rather than to start one from scratch. This decision falls in the realm of the art of purchasing a going-concern. When buying a going-concern, you will have to be twice as careful as if you were starting a new business.

One of the first questions you must ask when buying an existing business is, why is it being sold? The reasons provided by the vendor must not only be justifiable but must be rationalized along the lines of future viability. The past performance of the business must be of little importance to the buyer. The fact that Merlene Ottey is one of the most decorated female athletes in the world, does not guarantee her future value. It is whether she can continue to give a good performance on the track that is important. Buying a business is an investment and investment is about the future. You invest today because you are looking for a return in the future that will justify your investment today. That is the basic premise that you should keep in mind when making investment decisions. It does not matter whether it is large or small.

Regardless of what the books will show about past revenues and profits of the business, the future sales and profits are what should matter. We are quite aware of the use to which information about past performance could be put. However, that is just the beginning. Ultimately, it is what you see coming at you that you will use to make a final decision on whether to buy. Do not allow your judgment to be obscured by past financial and marketing performances of the going concern.

In addition to the above, here are some other questions that you should bring into your analytical machine;

      a. Is it possible that the current owner may set up a similar business in close proximity?

      b. Are there any legal constraints that could prevent you from continuing the business?

      c. Are there any threats to the business in the near future?

      d. What are the chances that the investment will not go bad?

      e. How long will it take to make back the money invested (payback period)?

      f. What are the industry prospects for the business?

      g. Are there any development plans that will negatively affect the business such as traffic changes or other government interventions?

What all of this is alluding to is that before you buy a business, make sure you open the bag and look inside. You may have to go a bit further to make sure that the animal you ordered is not only in the bag, but that it is alive and healthy.

A seller will tell you amazing things about the business that is to be sold. My question to such a seller would be, if the business is so successful why are you selling it?

> ### RULE # 23: WORD OF MOUTH IS THE WEAKEST FORM OF GUARANTEE; PUT YOUR DEALS IN BLACK AND WHITE.

While word of mouth makes one of the most effective means of advertising, it does not stand up to scrutiny when financial deals are being made. Financial transactions involve liquidity that if not carefully handled could go down the drain. Many small business operators in this country like to do business by word-of-mouth. This is a bad practice and it could just take one serious blunder to jeopardize the business forever. When you get a loan from the bank you have to sign for it. To get any form of utility service, one must first sign a document. Why then when some persons do business they do not want to do so formally? This is a very unsystematic practice and should be discouraged at all times.

It is not good enough that you put together a document for a business transaction. The document should spell out all the terms and conditions. A business deal is not secured if it is filled with ambiguity and loopholes. This will only expose the business to unnecessary risks. Even if the risks are not against you, such carelessness could see your business fighting lawsuits in the courts and in the long run, your business could lose a lot more than you were trying to gain in the first place. Things such as employment, staff loans, suspensions, credit sales, business loans and exclusive arrangements with other businesses must all be by written contract professional done.

Business owners/managers, who do not like to document their business transactions, have two basic reasons; either they are poor record keepers or they have ulterior motives not keeping records. Neither of those reasons is justifiable. If the deal cannot be recorded, keep it out of the business, otherwise, properly document it.

RULE # 24: DO NOT KEEP MORE CASH ON HAND THAN YOU NEED TO.

In our own businesses, we practise cash budgeting on a very strict basis. At the beginning of the year, we do a monthly cash budget, forecasted over 12 months. Each month, we will spend according to the budget and at the end of the month a variance report is done. With this approach, we will know how much cash we need to keep on hand and in the current account of the business. All extra cash will then be invested in short-term instruments or used in other areas of financial opportunities.

In order to abide by this rule, your first responsibility should be to determine how much cash you need to keep. This is where cash budgeting comes into full play. However, budgeting for cash is not as easy as it seems. The cash budget is one of the most difficult budgets you will have to construct and there are many factors upon which its construction relies. The following list represents the most critical of these factors;

a. The mode of financing your business
b. The size of your business, in respect of staff, production output/sales, etc.
c. The level and nature of sales
d. The level and nature of purchases
e. Industry factor such as sales
f. Marketing activities
g. Competition in the industry
h. The economic environment and its effect on the projections.

Your cash flow has two main elements to it, the inflows and the outflows. The aim of cash budgeting is to balance the inflows with the outflows so as to avoid cash shortages and surpluses. Where your cash budget shows that you may have a cash shortfall you will take the necessary steps to avoid this. On the other hand, where you see that you are going to have a massive cash surplus over a prolonged period (say 3 - 6 months) you will need to have a plan for that surplus. You should not have surplus cash sitting in a current account not earning anything. This is one of the more common mistakes made by small business operators. The basic principle behind a good cash management policy is that you must maximize earnings from your cash. Cash should always be working hard for the business.

Cash on hand includes all cash available to the business either by being able to draw a regular cheque or ready cash on location. Cash in a regular savings account may be included if it is the name of the business.

RULE # 25: DO NOT CONDUCT ALL YOUR BUSINESSES WITH ONE BANK.

If you break this rule it would be like putting all your eggs in one basket. If you check around you would find that all big businesses have multiple accounts, not only in one bank but also in different banks. The reasons for this approach to banking are varied.

    a. Banks offer different services to their customers

    b. It facilitates services to staff, customers and suppliers (distribution of service)

    c. It reduces the risk to the business in case one of the banks should fall into problems

    d. It facilitates cash inflow from the payments of your customers

This approach to banking is considered prudent financial management and should be practised by all businesses. In the mid-90s a number of businesses were wiped out because all their accounts were kept at a number of failed banks. It is documented in a story called the "Finsac Catastrophe".

RULE # 26: ALWAYS PUT IN PLACE, A CONTINGENCY FINANCIAL PLAN.

No business plan is perfect. The financial plan is the most susceptible to deviations. If your sales fall below target by 20% it could affect your debt repayment, your monthly salaries or it could send you back to a lending institution to borrow more money. Even before you go into business you should expect these things. The fact that you expected these possibilities you should take steps to reduce the adverse effects should these expectations be realised.

How does one put in place a financial plan B? First you have to go back to plan A, and look at it analytically to see the potential problems and the sources of these problems. Having identified the source of potential problems, you now have to create preventative measures. What are some of the potential financial problems that a business, especially a new one may encounter? Here is a small list;

1. Undercapitalization
2. Cash shortage
3. Lower than projected sales
4. Too much debt (high debt ratio)

In business, there is no place for complacency. You really have to look at your business plan and be cognizant of the possibility of these events. What if there is a cash shortage? What If this should happen and it is due to the rapid growth of the business, you may want to ensure that you have a backup prospect for finding equity to finance this growth. Just the same way you should have a plan to offset the effects of poor sales revenues and a high debt ratio.

Ironically, the main aspect of any backup financial plan for your business is the initial financial plan, so make sure you have a good one to start with.

RULE # 27: DO NOT OVERDO YOUR COST REDUCTION AND PROFIT MAXIMIZATION ACTIVITIES.

In a bid to cut cost and to maximize profits, some businesses cut all kinds of corners that eventually hurt the business, the customers or both. Some of the activities that managers resort to include;

1. Increasing the product prices
2. Reducing package size
3. Cutting staff to reduce payroll cost
4. Reduction in the quality of products
5. Increasing production output
6. Reduced advertising and other marketing acitvities

When you do these things make sure your customers and your business do not become the victims. The fact of the matter is that these policies sometimes have a good short term effect but long- term disasters.

Cutting advertising is one of the most dangerous things you can do for your business. Advertising is your main contact with old and new customers. You are always trying to grow your business and if you cut advertising, you could be slowing your sales, effectively bringing your business to a halt or a slower rate of growth.

RULE # 28: TAXATION SHOULD BE AN INTEGRAL PART OF YOUR FINANCIAL PLAN.

One of the biggest fears among small business operators is taxation. Taxation is an inescapable obligation/outflow and should be treated as such. In that regard, you will have to factor taxation into the financial plan of your business. We have alluded to this earlier.

There are basically three types of taxes that you will have to contend with, sales tax (GCT), income tax and statutory deductions/payments. There are some special taxes which may come into play as the government sees fit.

Sales taxes are collected entirely on behalf of the government. Depending on the size (turnover) of your business, you may have to pay over this money to the Inland Revenue Department monthly or bi-monthly. Income tax, on the other hand, is a tax based on profit levels. Personal income tax is based on your total income less deductibles. Corporation tax is based on the profits of the business less expenses. Statutory fees and payroll taxes are those fixed or variable fees payable to the government based on some predetermined legislations and formulas. These include payment for the various types of licenses, property taxes, housing trust matching deductions, etc. While some statutory fees are fixed in value, others such as payroll taxes are based on the size of the payroll. Your employment decisions must, therefore, be guided by the rules that govern these taxes.

The importance of taxation to the financial operation of the business has to do not only with the timing but also the size of the payouts. These payouts involve cash and as such proper budgeting must be in place to ensure that when these payments are made the business does not suffer a cash shortage.

Taxation also has implications for profitability. There are times when businesses have to pay the taxes by taking an overdraft (Loan). This means that interest expenses will be incurred and will therefore adversely affect profit. It is even worse if your taxes are overdue and you have to pay penalties. I must point out here, however, that a number of businesses will take the risk of not paying the taxes on time because the alternative for which the cash is used may yield enough benefit to offset the cost. This is risky financial management and it should not be encouraged.

Another good reason for the inclusion of taxation in financial management is when it concerns investment strategies. There are times when taxation policies are designed to either encourage or discourage investment in some sectors. Most times these policies affect investment options such as short-term securities and the stock market. One sector in which the policy difference is very clear is agriculture. Income tax is exempt for a business that has approved farming status. Also, in the area of information technology (IT) the government gives favourable considerations to the investment in equipment. The rate of depreciation (more appropriately capital allowances) favours the bottom line and is a serious consideration for profitability planning.

The acquisition of assets by a business can be by direct purchase, lease or loan. When you take a loan, only the interest and the loan processing fees can be applied against your profit in calculating taxable profit. A lease on a capital item is, however, written off against income, thus allowing for a less tax liability.

Obviously, there is a lot to gain from given proper considerations to taxation in financial management. However, taxation is both a legal and an accounting matter. You must, therefore, endeavour to consult with your tax advisor or accountant before you make key financial decisions. It pays to have a good accountant, who knows taxes, for your business.

RULE # 29: DO NOT USE CASH FROM THE BUSINESS TO INDULGE IN PERSONAL ASSET ACCUMULATION.

This is one of the most difficult rules to obey in Jamaica. The breaking of this rule is responsible for some of the worse business failures in this country. Just what do we mean by the rule? Simply put, do not use the cash from the business to buy personal items such as fancy cars, home entertainment systems and other items of pure personal worth. The money is for the business not for you. No business can survive under that kind of fiscal indiscipline. You may be thinking that if the business is yours then the cash is yours. Not so. The business is supposed to be an entity separate from you. Just the same way your dog has its own identity your business has its own identity. How then do you get around the problem of squeezing the cash from the business?

Let us start with a prudent question. What do you do when you employ a person to manage your business? You pay the person a salary. That is exactly what you should do for yourself, take a salary. This salary amount should not be any arbitrary amount. It should be commensurate with what your market worth is. If you over pay yourself this would be tantamount to breaking the rule.

Let us further explore some of the implications of breaking the rule. In a business that is making a profit, pulling out cash would erode the capital base. You are effective engaged in profit taking when you may not even be sure the business is making a profit. If a time should come when you need a strong capital base the business could be wiped out of existence by one of two means. Firstly, you may have to borrow money to prop up the base and this could lead to bankruptcy. Secondly, the business could die from the lack of investment because there is no money to invest. One classic example of this kind of stupidity is the case in which a man takes the cash from his business and builds a house.

When the business becomes strapped for cash he borrows money from a lending institution, using the house as collateral and then he defaults on the loan. In the short run, the lending institution will have to realize the collateral and the business goes under. There are just too many stories like this; the lesson is very easy to learn. At all times, you should plough back a reasonable portion of the profit into the business. This will allow the business to grow and ultimately become a big business. The very large businesses that you see today did not start big, they simply followed the rules.

It is best to wait until the business has good profits that are available to shareholders at the appropriate times.

RULE # 30: YOU SHOULD NOT TRY TO RUN A BUSINESS WITHOUT AN ACCOUNTANT.

We are not accountants but we have enough experience to know that one of the three most important people in the life of a businessman is an accountant. The other two are a doctor and a lawyer. Your wife/husband goes without saying.

Who is the accountant? He/she is the person who is responsible for one of the most important roles in the business, record keeping and in many cases, financial planning. The accountant will provide you with some of the most important pieces of information that you will need to make financial decisions. Nonetheless, the accountant should not be abused. You may be surprised to see that statement but let us explain. When you employ the services of your accountant outside of scope of the employment, you are abusing the post. A number of businesses that we know, including large ones, pass on the responsibility of developing the financial forecast to the sole responsibility of the accountant. This is an abuse of the post and is definitely wrong. The foundation of any business plan or financial performance forecast is the sales forecast. This is a marketing function. If you do not have someone in charge of marketing, it will become your responsibility to forecast sales. This can be a collaborative effort between you and your staff. Nonetheless, it is a marketing exercise. Once the sales foundation is laid, the accountant can go ahead to forecast the financial plan.

There have been many cases wherein the annual budget for a business is laid down and the marketing person is not even involved in the development of the plan. We will say to you, the absurdity of running a business in such a manner, peaks in that kind of situation.

Another way in which the post of the accountant is abused is by allowing the accountant to manage the business. This is terribly wrong. This can lead to catastrophic consequences. Even if you are an accountant, you should not do the books for your own business. It may be difficult to adhere to these principles but when you rationally consider the situations in their entirety, you will have to come to the same conclusion.

RULE # 31: AT THE END OF A FINANCIAL YEAR DO NOT PAY OUT ALL YOUR PROFITS TO THE BUSINESS OWNERS/SHAREHOLDERS.

Naturally if you are running a limited liability company it may not be so difficult to follow this rule. However, if it is a small family business, it could be difficult. Before attempting to get into details let us first explain the rule.

At the end of a financial period, the accountant would have produced a financial report. The elements of this report are an income statement

(Profit and loss statement), a balance sheet (statement of financial position) and possibly a use of funds statement. The smaller the business the less likely that you will have a funds flow statement.

Having produced these statements and assuming that a profit is made, you will have to decide how much of the profit, if any, to pay to the owners of the business. The situation becomes less complicated when you are the only owner (sole trader) of the business. Should you pay 25%, 50% or 75% of the profit? To answer this question you have to look at a number of factors as outlined below;

a. Is the profit of the business liquid profit That is, although you have a profit do you have that profit in cash? If you do not have it in cash then you cannot pay out any dividend to the owners.

c. If you have cash but there is a plan for the business to invest in a very profitable venture, you may not want to pay out too much cash. If you pay out too much cash you may have to borrow that money later on. That will cost the business more and cut into its profit for the following year.

d. The future growth of the business will depend greatly on the availability of capital, particularly low-cost capital. A cash payment from profit will provide encouragement for the owners to pump more money into the business if this should be needed in the future.

e. Another thing to consider is taxation. Since the dividends will be subjected to personal income tax, it may just be prudent enough to leave the cash in retained earnings so that the business can invest this which in the long term will work out better for all concerned.

Whatever the payout decision, it should not jeopardize the cash or the future investment viability of the business. There are times when you have to postpone a payment in order to secure the business for the long term. There may be persons who may not agree with such a decision but it is just business. Like plants, a business needs a certain environment in which to grow and be profitable. If you upset this environment the business may just die from the disequilibrium.

RULE # 32: OWNERSHIP (BUYING) OF ASSETS DOES NOT ALWAYS YIELD THE BEST FINANCIAL RESULTS.

A business can acquire the assets it needs by renting/hiring, leasing and direct purchase. The decision regarding acquisition that you ultimately make will depend on the availability of funds, cost, period of use and the comparative cost. This rule is broken by many small businesses and has put them in dire financial positions. Let us now explain fully what we mean by this very important rule.

If you are into construction you may find it necessary to clear land in order to start you planned construction. The clearing of the land may require a tractor or a backhoe. It does not necessarily mean that you need to purchase a D9 or a brand new backhoe in order to get the job done. You can simply rent one for a day or two. In any case, you will be passing on the cost to the client for whom you are doing the work.

Let use another example. You operate a small film company and you are given a contract to shoot a commercial. Based on the quality of the commercial requested, you realise you will have to get a 4K camera. Do you call up B&H Photo Video in New York and ask them how much for a Red Epic camera? You don't. You can simply rent one right here in Jamaica for a day or two. A Red Epic will run you USD 30,000 (at the time of writing) just for the basic camera. You have to invest a whole lot more just to use the camera and to be able to edit the footage that you get from shooting with it.

Hopefully the point is now clear. You need not own all the assets that you need in your business. To decide on whether to buy depends on a whole set of factors include frequency of use, the cost of maintenance, the cost of the asset and alternative cost of acquisition such as leasing and renting. The decision must be made based on how it will affect your financial position, mainly your profitability.

RULE # 33: LOOK TO INSURANCE FOR THE FINANCIAL SAFETY OF YOUR BUSINESS.

Jamaica is a country where many do not have a strong appreciation for insurance. In some cases where insurance is a statutory requirement, it is not present. Insurance can be a very helpful element in your financial plan and there are many kinds of insurance that a small business operator may want to consider for the business.

In a number of small businesses, there are persons that are very important to the business, persons without whom the business cannot operate. In such cases, it may be a good idea to have key man insurance for such persons.

In other situation such as with entertainment businesses and restaurant, public liability insurance can give you a good cushion against lawsuits should such come into consideration for whatever reason. Other forms of insurance that a small business needs to consider include the insurance of staff, particularly those involved in high-risk activities, event insurance and the insurance of assets. Too often we hear about a fire where all the assets of the business are destroyed.

Insurance may seem like useless expenses to many persons. However, such thoughts are fueled by ignorance and inexperience and should not be accommodated. It is a good idea to speak to an insurance expert at the time you are considering setting up your business.

Conclusion

The foregoing rules were provided for your guidance and for a more effective management of your business. We understand that rules are made to be broken, however, it is our sincere wish that you break the rules with caution and a pragmatic understanding of the consequences of your actions.

Finance is needed to start the business, provide the fuel that will enable it to grow, expand and serve as the yardstick to measure the health of the company. Every aspect of the business depends on finance. It will be required to hire needed personnel, purchase equipment and raw materials. The rate of growth and expansion of the business will significantly depend on the availability of finance, the nature of the sources of finance and the cost of capital. Proper management of the financial portfolio will allow the business to take advantage of investment opportunities that may be present in the business environment.

The primary means of short term finance for small business operation are sales and loans. Commercial banks provide not just working capital for business but also other facilities and services that are vital for the day to day financial operation of the business. Although commercial banks provide many solutions there are many problems that lurk in the dark realities of financial carelessness and errors. One must therefore be prudent in these matters if one is to avoid these pitfalls.

Another integral aspect of your business is marketing. You will need to let potential customers know about your products and services; this is accomplished through marketing; without it, customers will not be aware of your product and services. Marketing, to a great extent, drives the activities of the other departments of the business. It is marketing that will determine if a sufficient demand exists to make the product/service profitable to undertake the research, development and production. It, therefore, stands at the very core of your business success. It cannot be overstated that as a business operator you need to pay close attention to these areas of your operation.

Small businesses have a number of important advantages that allow them to grow and serve the market. Marketing however, has a symbiotic relationship with finance. In order to kick start and continue the marketing process, finance must be in place to fuel the resources needed for the marketing function. It is lack of knowledge of this functional connectivity between finance and marketing that sometimes lead to week business decisions and subsequent failures.

With the recognition of the short coming in marking for many small businesses, we have developed a practical text on small business marketing in Jamaica.

In order to get the 411 on small business marketing in Jamaica, you will be well served to get a copy of the next text, **"The Rules of Marketing for Small Businesses"**.

Paul O. Beale – Creative Entrepreneur

Paul O. Beale has been involved in the creative industry for over 32 years. His involvement includes writing and directing plays, TV dramas, screen plays, writing books and the creation of theatrical characters. Beale's successes in the creative industry are largely based on the creation of stage and screen characters such as Big Pants, Delcita Coldwater, Melcita Esconbar, The Handicap, Mrs. Blouse, Elizabeth Sight, Icilda Coldwater, Stamma, Jooky Jam, the Maama Man, Mr. Don Paper, Ras I-Maan-I and others.

Inspired by the remarkable success of comic strips characters such as Spiderman, Superman, King Kong, Batman, et al, he set out in 1985 to be the first to take up that challenge as a creative force in driving the Jamaican theatre and film sector through the creation of unique characters. This entrepreneurial endeavour has built a strong foundation for him over the years. His characters are now known throughout the Jamaican Diaspora.

The creative endeavours such as that undertaken by Beale, et al are not seen as good business ventures. However, creativity can be one of the most profitable for of entrepreneurship. It is also one of the sectors in which Jamaica can gain a bit of competitive advantage and global recognition. We would like to implore business owners and operators to support and get involved in the creative industry so that the opportunities locked in the sector can be made available for profitable investment opportunities.

Creativity features largely in product development, promotion and entertainment; one of the largest industries on the world. We are now making moves in film making and this is another area where small business operators may look for growth and expansion through collaborations and strategic alliances. Examples are all around us and Paul O. Beale has demonstrated the possibility of such undertaking by the creation of Pragmatic Productions Limited, a company he incorporated in 2011. Pragmatic Productions is now responsible for the production of TV programmes such as **JOINT TENANTS (39 episodes), the enTRAPreneur (26 episodes) and BLOODLINE.**

www.ingramcontent.com/pod-product-compliance
Lightning Source LLC
Chambersburg PA
CBHW070328190526
45169CB00005B/1795